GymnStars Volume 12

SUNI LEE

GOLDEN TRAILBLAZER

BY CHRISTINE DZIDRUMS

SUNI LEE

GOLDEN TRAILBLAZER

BY CHRISTINE DZIDRUMS

GymnStars Volume 12

Creative Media Pubishing

CREATIVE MEDIA, INC.
Whittier, California
United States of America

www.creativemedia.net

Cover photo by Ricardo Bufolin
Book & cover design by Joseph Dzidrums

First Edition: November 2021

ATOS Book Level: 6.3
AR Points: 1

LCCN: On file

ISBN: 978-1-950298-09-9
eISBN: 978-1-950298-10-5
hcISBN: 978-1-950298-11-2

**For
*Josh, Timmy, and Ashley***

Table of Contents

"I hope I can inspire people."

Sunisa Lee paced anxiously. What was taking so long?

The 18-year-old gymnast waited for the scoreboard to post the final standings. She had just unleashed four strong routines in the biggest competition of her life, the women's gymnastics all-around at the 2020 Toyko Olympics. Would she become the fifth straight American woman to capture gold in the event, or would she settle for the silver medal?

Rebeca Andrade had just delivered a strong floor exercise performance. If the judges awarded her routine with marks higher than 13.801, the competitor from Brazil would take gold. Anything lower than that? Suni would become the Olympic all-around gold medalist.

Suni held her breath as the scoreboard dimmed for a second before flashing 13.666 on its screen. Rebeca's score was good, but it wasn't good enough. She would take home the silver medal.

Suni Lee was golden!

The eighteen-year-old squealed with delight. She jumped up and down in excitement and hugged her longtime coach, Jess Graba.

Millions of people around the world had watched Suni deliver four stellar routines to win the gold medal. As a result, little girls everywhere suddenly dreamed of becoming the next Suni Lee.

Following her victory, Suni's face was plastered on the front page of countless newspapers. Her *Instagram* account shot up to over one million followers. News outlets from across the globe clamored to interview the teenager.

Suni Lee had become a bona fide celebrity, and the public clamored to learn more about her. Who was gymnastics newest star?

Before Suni became a household name champion, she was a teenager from South St. Paul, Minnesota, with dreams of competing at the Olympics in gymnastics.

To better appreciate Suni's difficult road to gold, one must learn her parents' story first.

When Yeev Thoj was twelve years old, her family left Laos to live in the United States. Laos was home to many Hmong people, like the Thojs. Hmong is an ethnic group, mainly from Vietnam, Laos, Thailand, Myanmar, and southern China, that fought alongside the United States in the Vietnam War.

Yeev's family settled in St. Paul, Minnesota, for a specific reason. The state capital had the largest concentration of Hmong in the United States. The Thojs loved their new home.

"We went to a grocery store, and I thought it was magic," Yeev told *ESPN.* "Vanilla ice cream in a box. Starburst. And girls wore jeans instead of skirts. I was so excited to wear jeans."

Yeev remained in the St. Paul area when she reached adulthood. She settled into a career as a health care worker.

On March 9, 2003, in South St. Paul, Minnesota, Yeev gave birth to a beautiful baby girl. The new mother named her daughter Sunisa Phabsomphou. Her child was named after her favorite Thai soap opera star.

Two years after her daughter's birth, Yeev met John Lee, a divorcee and single father. John had two children of his own, a son named Jonah and a daughter, Shyenne.

Like Yeev, John was of Hmong descent. He had also immigrated to America with his parents during his childhood.

When Yeev and John fell in love, their two families merged into one. Once an only child, Sunisa suddenly found herself living with two new siblings. She loved having a new sister in Shyenne, who was only 12 days older than her.

Sunisa adored her new father. He was a loving man and a fun, playful person. She was so thrilled when he adopted her that she took his last name.

And so, Sunisa Phabsomphou became Sunisa Lee.

St. Paul, Minnesota: Birthplace of Sunisa Lee

"It just came natural to me."

Over the next few years, the Lee household expanded. Yeev and John welcomed three children together: Evionn, Lucky, and Noah. The couple had six children in all!

Sunisa, Suni for short, was an active child with endless energy. One day her mom took her to a park so she could play. When Suni taught herself somersaults, a family friend suggested gymnastics classes for the young girl.

Why not? Yeev thought. After all, it would be good exercise for her daughter and a good way to burn off her energy.

Suni was enrolled in a gymnastics class for toddlers. She was always excited to head to the gym. She would tumble on the foam mat for hours if it were possible.

At home, Suni loved showing off new gymnastics skills she'd learned. She could do cartwheels, somersaults, and backflips.

"She was addicted to doing backflips," Yeev told *Bleacher Report.*

Sometimes, the rambunctious child even used her bed mattress as a trampoline. Although, her parents didn't like it when she did that!

When Suni was just six years old, she began taking classes at Midwest Gymnastics. The 30,000 square-foot facility was located in Moscow, Minnesota.

Initially, Suni took lessons with a man named Punnarith Koy. Her first coach taught her the fundamentals of gymnastics, and he was surprised by how quickly his young student learned new skills.

Suni fell in love with gymnastics and couldn't satisfy her hunger for the sport. On non-gymnastics days, she begged her parents to drive her to the gym so she could practice. Most of the time, she preferred going to gymnastics classes to playing with her friends.

Suni often wished she could practice gymnastics at home. There was only one problem. She didn't have the necessary equipment.

At the gym, Suni loved mounting the balance beam and performing tricks on the four-inch-wide apparatus. Eventually, her father built her a balance beam in their backyard, so she could practice whenever she wanted.

Suni's athletic father could do backflips, like his daughter. So, the two often performed synchronized flips together. Sometimes, they even did backflips into the pool.

By age seven, Suni began turning heads at Midwest Gymnastics. The young girl was fearless with a natural talent for the sport. She could perform difficult skills that older, more experienced gymnasts couldn't do.

One day, Suni caught the attention of Jess Graba, the owner of Midwest Gymnastics. Jess ran the gym with his wife and coaching partner, Alison Lim.

"It was super raw, and she was just a little kid, but she had some talent," Jess later told *Elle Magazine*.

Jess and Alison became Suni's primary coaches. Over the years, the young gymnast grew close to the husband-and-wife team and regarded them as parental figures.

14-year-old Suni competes at the 2017 U.S. Classic.

Around the same time, Suni began competing in gymnastics meets. During the events, she performed routines on four apparatuses: balance beam, floor exercise, uneven bars, and vault.

At only her second competition ever, Suni won Minnesota's state all-around title. It was quickly becoming apparent to all that the young girl possessed a remarkable talent.

At first, Suni disliked competitions. They made her nervous. But over time, she grew to enjoy them because they helped her express her feelings when words didn't sometimes work so well.

When Suni was nine years old, she watched the gymnastics events at the 2012 London Olympics. She admired the American team dubbed the Fierce Five. The youngster cheered when Gabby Douglas, McKayla Maroney, Aly Raisman, Kyla Ross, and Jordyn Wieber became only the second U.S. women's gymnastics squad to win team gold.

A few days later, Suni watched in awe as Gabby Douglas won a second gold medal in the women's all-around competition. In gymnastics' premiere event, each competitor performs a routine on the four apparatuses: balance beam, floor exercise, uneven bars, and vault. The gymnast with the highest total earns the esteemed title of the best all-around gymnast.

Suni also cheered when Aly Raisman captured gold on the floor exercise, and McKayla Maroney took silver on the vault.

After the London Games ended, Suni re-watched the five gymnasts' routines over and over on *YouTube*. Then one day while watching one of the videos, Suni had a life-changing realization. Someday, she wanted to compete at the Olympics, too.

It was time to put her plan into action!

"Gymnastics is really fun and challenging in a good way."

Suni couldn't satisfy her appetite for gymnastics. So, when she wasn't tumbling or vaulting or swinging from the uneven bars, she watched older gymnastics videos on *YouTube*.

Suni really loved watching clips of 2008 Olympians Nastia Liukin and Shawn Johnson. Although the athletes had vastly different gymnastics styles, Suni found qualities to appreciate in both gymnasts. She admired Nastia's lyrical lines, and she liked Shawn's explosive tumbling.

Before one meet, Suni's father had an interesting proposal for her. If she won the all-around gold medal, he would buy her a new iPhone.

An eager Suni accepted the challenge. She'd wanted a new phone for months and felt determined to win one. Sure enough, she nabbed the gold medal at the competition. A few days later, she received her new iPhone.

In 2016, Suni became a junior elite gymnast. The move made her eligible to compete at the U.S. Championships with the best gymnasts in the country. She could also be selected to represent the United States in international competitions, like her heroes, the Fierce Five.

"As soon as I decided that's what I wanted to do, I really started focusing on it and putting a bunch of training hours in," she told the *St. Paul Pioneer Press*.

In early June, Suni competed at the 2016 U.S. Classic as a junior. On the senior level, Simone Biles and Aly Raisman were the event's headliners.

Before the competition, Suni began doubting her ability. Did she belong with the country's best junior gymnasts?

Fortunately, Suni's father gave excellent pep talks. By the time he finished assuring his daughter that she was as talented as the other gymnasts, she felt pumped to compete.

Ultimately, Suni struggled somewhat in her first elite event. However, she gained valuable experience while competing with America's other top gymnasts. She couldn't wait to go home and learn new skills.

A few weeks later, Suni watched excitedly as Simone Biles, Gabby Douglas, Laurie Hernandez, Madison Kocian, and Aly Raisman represented the United States in women's gymnastics at the 2016 Olympics. Dubbed the Final Five, the Americans snagged a victory in the team event. Meanwhile, Simone Biles collected additional gold medals in the all-around, floor, and vault competitions.

When the 2016 Olympics drew to a close, sports fans began counting down to the next games in Tokyo, Japan.

"Tokyo has been one of my biggest goals for so long and still is," Suni told a reporter.

In March 2017, Suni traveled to Montreal, Canada, for the competition, International Gymnix. Her teammates included Emma Malabuyo, Maile O'Keefe, and Gabby Perea.

Despite their inexperience on the international scene, the Americans worked well as a unit. They delivered strong performances and won the team competition. Italy finished second, and Russia placed third.

To her delight, Suni won a second shiny souvenir in Canada. She captured a silver medal on the uneven bars.

Young Suni competes as a junior at the 2018 U.S. Gymnastics Championships.

In mid-August, Suni flew to Anaheim, California, to compete at the 2017 U.S. Championships. She improved her placements from the previous year. Her highlights included 8th in the all-around and 5th in the floor exercise.

For the 2018 season, Suni remained a junior-level gymnast again. Her strong efforts at the Pacific Rim Gymnastics Championships helped lead the American junior girls to a team silver medal. Meanwhile, she finished second on vault, balance beam, and floor.

In mid-August, Suni arrived in Boston, Massachusetts, for the 2018 U.S. Championships. The historic TD Garden, home to NHL's Boston Bruins and the NBA's Boston Celtics, served as the host for the competition.

When Suni left Beantown one week later, she was the proud owner of an uneven bars gold medal and a bronze medal for the all-around event. Her impressive showing also landed her on the national team.

"It went pretty good," she told reporters. "I still have things to clean up, but I'm pretty proud of how I did overall."

When her lengthy season ended, Suni closed the door on her elite junior career. She felt satisfied with all she had accomplished at that level.

Looking ahead, Suni had lofty goals for her first senior season. She planned to execute a higher scoring vault and increase the difficulty of her tumbling. The determined teenager also wanted to prove that she was a serious contender for the Tokyo Olympics!

Bring on the senior ranks. Suni Lee was eager for a new challenge.

TM

TOKYO 2020

Tokyo 2020

"I don't want to let myself down."

On March 3, 2019, Suni kicked off her senior career with a spectacular showing at the Jesolo Trophy in Italy. She earned four gold medals: team, all-around, uneven bars, and floor exercise. Plus, she won a bronze on the balance beam.

Suni followed up her stunning senior debut with a silver medal on the balance beam at American Classic. Then, she nabbed a silver medal on the uneven bars at U.S. Classic.

A few weeks later, a family tragedy nearly derailed the gymnast's last half of the season.

On August 4, 2019, Suni's father was helping a neighbor trim his tree. Suddenly, he lost his balance and fell off a ladder. He was rushed to the hospital, where doctors told him that he was paralyzed from the waist down.

The accident occurred two days before Suni planned to leave for her first senior nationals. The devastated teenager wanted to withdraw from the competition. There would be other nationals, but she only had one father.

However, John wouldn't hear of Suni staying home. Instead, he encouraged his daughter to compete at the event and make her dreams come true.

"Just go," he told her. "Go do your thing."

Honoring her father's wish, Suni headed to Kansas City, Missouri, for the 2019 U.S. Championships. On the morning of the first day of the competition, her father FaceTimed her from his hospital bed.

"It doesn't matter where you place," he stressed. "Whether you win first or not, you're still number one in my book."

While at the competition, Suni didn't reveal her father's accident to anyone. She didn't want any distractions.

"I wasn't in the best place going into it," she admitted later. "But I switched gears and competed for my dad. I had to be the best I could be for my dad."

And she did exactly that.

The sixteen-year-old made a spectacular statement by winning the all-around silver medal behind her idol, Simone Biles. She also earned gold on the uneven bars and a bronze medal on floor exercise.

"It didn't surprise me that she was able to do it," Jess said afterward. "She's just a tough competitor, a tough kid."

"She rocked that competition," he added.

"Watching her was very emotional," recalled her sister Shyenne. "I knew she was thinking about my dad the entire time."

"Whatever she's doing is going to make my parents proud," she continued. "Because they sacrificed a lot to come here."

Suni was thrilled with her accomplishment. She had amassed a big medal haul at nationals.

"I proved to myself that I can do anything I want when I put my mind to it," she told *Bleacher Report*.

USA Gymnastics invited the new all-around silver medalist to attend the Worlds Team Selection Camp. The event determined which women would represent the United States at the 2019 World Championships in Germany.

Suni Lee was officially a contender for the world team!

Suni practices her beam routine.

"I try my best to have a good practice every day, because I know it's gonna set me up for a good competition."

Suni's gymnastics career kept her busy, but she found time to have fun, too. She enjoyed camping and fishing with her family. Like most teenagers, she texted with her friends a lot, too.

Of course, Suni's closest friend lived with her. Shyenne wasn't just her sister, she was her best friend. The two girls were always giggling over an inside joke or funny *YouTube* clips. Sometimes, they convinced their parents to take them to the drive-in to see the latest box office hit.

"I keep her life from being only gymnastics," Shyenne told *ESPN*. "I keep her social life active. I keep her normal."

Suni also liked using *Snapchat*, the multimedia messaging app. Thanks to her silly dance videos, she had accumulated a loyal following on the platform.

At the World Team Selection Camp, Suni proved that her U.S. Championships' performance was no fluke. She soared to another second-place finish in the all-around, behind Simone Biles. Plus, she won uneven bars and finished second on the balance beam and floor exercise.

At the end of camp, the world team was announced. The five gymnasts who would compose the American squad were: Simone Biles, Jade Carey, Kara Eaker, Suni Lee, and Grace McCallum.

Suni had booked a ticket to the world championships! She would be the youngest member on the American team.

In Germany, Suni soaked up her trip to the World Championships. She had worked so hard to make the world team, and she savored every second of it.

For starters, she enjoyed getting to know her teammates. She bonded quickly with all of them.

"I'm feeling amazing," she said. "It feels surreal, and it feels amazing to be able to compete with such an amazing group of girls and with such amazing gymnasts all around me."

In the team final, Suni competed on three events: balance beam, floor exercise, and uneven bars. At the end of the competition, the Americans clinched the gold medal by over five points ahead of second-place finishers, Russia. Meanwhile, Italy collected the bronze medal.

"It feels so amazing to be a world champion," she gushed afterward. "I still can't believe it."

The competition hadn't concluded, though. Suni had qualified for three individual events: all-around, uneven bars, and floor exercise.

After placing eighth in the all-around, Suni focused on the uneven bars event. Her routine was packed with difficulty. If she completed it flawlessly, she'd almost certainly win a medal. Looking like a seasoned competitor, she executed a strong program that earned the bronze medal.

"I wanted to medal so badly, and it feels absolutely amazing," she confessed.

Suni took part in the floor exercise finals next. Thanks to a strong effort, she scooped up a silver medal behind Simone Biles. It felt surreal to stand on the medal podium next to her hero.

"Simone is very inspiring," she raved. "She has helped me get through this competition."

With the 2019 season in the books, Suni looked ahead to 2020. She was a strong contender to make the United States women's gymnastics team at the Olympics in Tokyo. The teenager planned to earn a plane ticket to Japan!

Suni competes at the 2019 World Gymnastics Championships.

"Mentally it's [the pandemic] helped because it makes me want this even more."

In early 2020, a global pandemic shook the world. COVID-19, a highly contagious respiratory disease that spread rapidly, caused millions of deaths across the globe.

Businesses and schools shut down as medical professionals urged people to quarantine at home. In the meantime, scientists worked frantically to find a vaccine to battle the deadly virus.

On March 20, 2020, the International Olympic Committee announced the postponement of the Tokyo Games.

Although most agreed that the postponement of the Olympics was a wise decision, Suni still felt devastated by the news. She immediately broke down in tears.

"To have that taken away from us without having any control was very hard," she admitted.

When Suni texted Jess to express her disappointment, he told her to cry if she felt like it. She shouldn't hold in her emotions.

Suni fell into a depressed state, which she found difficult to shake. She slept a lot. When she was awake, doubts about her competitive future nagged. Did she even want to continue with gymnastics? Would she ever return to her peak shape after missing so much training time?

Sadly, COVID-19 hit Suni's family hard when her aunt and uncle contracted the disease. She was devastated when the virus claimed her aunt's life.

"She was one of my favorite aunts because she was so loving and caring and was always supportive of me," Suni told *The New York Times*.

At first, it seemed like Suni's uncle would be okay. He seemed to be recovering from COVID-19. Then thirteen days after his wife's death, he suffered a fatal heart attack.

Losing both beloved family members gutted Suni. Her aunt and uncle had been a constant presence in her life. They often babysat her when she was a little girl. Her uncle even used his vast knowledge of herbal medicines to help her heal injuries throughout the years.

Typically, Hmong funerals stretch over two to three days. When someone dies, mourners make small money boats from gold or silver paper that provide wealth for the spiritual journey of the deceased.

Due to COVID-19 concerns, Suni could not attend her aunt's and uncle's funerals. So instead, she devoted an entire day to folding little boats in her loved one's honor.

Suni surfs the internet.

On May 25, 2020, police officers in Minneapolis were filmed using excessive force while arresting a 46-year-old African-American man named George Floyd, who died during the interaction.

Throughout the country, people gathered to protest police officers' treatment of black civilians. Many demonstrations took place in Minnesota, where Floyd's death had occurred.

However, the protests led to the vandalization of stores in the Minneapolis area. When some of the unrest happened near the Lee's home, John urged his family to stay indoors until the chaos settled.

"The protests in Minneapolis were really crazy for everyone here," Suni told *The New York Times*. "I didn't go to the protests, but I understand where the anger is coming from and why people are trying to push for change."

To worsen matters, a strong anti-Asian sentiment also permeated throughout the United States. As a result, many Asian Americans found themselves as the target of random attacks.

"People hate on us for no reason," Suni told *Elle Magazine*. "It would be cool to show that we are more than what they say."

Suni's heart and spirit felt broken. More than ever, she had doubts about her gymnastics future. The seventeen-year-old confided to her parents that she was considering quitting gymnastics.

Suni's mother and father encouraged Suni to keep going. The Olympics were likely to take place the following summer. Why abandon her dream when it was so close?

Suni mulled over her folks' advice and realized they were right. She didn't want to live with any regret later. She would stick it out another year.

Slowly, Suni emerged from her depression. The resolute gymnast did presses and handstands at home and scheduled workouts with her coaches over *Zoom*. Plus, she ran four miles every day to keep in shape.

Suni also chatted with her teammates through texts and *Snapchat*. Discussing her disappointment over the postponement of the Olympics with other athletes helped her feel less alone.

Simone Biles became one of the girls that Suni talked to a lot. The two discussed everything from manicures to house hunting.

"It's really nice to get to know her in this way," Suni told *The New York Times*. "She was my idol. I used to see her as this intimidating gold medalist, but now she's a friend."

After a while, Suni viewed the postponement in a positive light. She'd use the extra year to improve her consistency and upgrade her routines.

The pandemic also let Suni spend quality time with her sister, Shyenne. The two teenagers loved experimenting with the latest makeup and hairstyle trends. Suni even asked her sibling to apply eyelash extensions on top of her existing eyelashes.

The sisters took their driver's license test, too. After passing the exam, they were thrilled with the newfound independence it brought them.

Suni was also heartened when her father's physical condition kept improving. In particular, he saw significant improvement in the use of his hands.

During the pandemic, Suni made a monumental decision regarding her future. She signed a national letter of intent with Auburn University. The gymnast accepted a full scholarship from the college and would compete in NCAA gymnastics.

Head coach of the Auburn gymnastics team? Jeff Graba, twin brother of her coach Jess.

Suni looked forward to immersing herself in the college environment. The teenager had missed many typical teenage experiences over the years due to her training schedule. So, she planned to soak up every second at Auburn University.

"I do want to go to college and have fun and kind of get away from this elite atmosphere because it's so crazy," she remarked. "I know that college is going to be way better."

Eventually, the quarantine ended. Midwest Gymnastics reopened, and the Olympics were rescheduled for 2021. Suni felt optimistic and excited about the following year.

"I fought off the negative thoughts and the sadness, and just focused," she recalled. "Now I feel tougher because of it."

Auburn University

"I'm not going to give up until I make the Olympic team."

Suni felt excited to return to her home gym. The elite athlete welcomed a return to normalcy. She began training again under the guidance of her coaches.

Unfortunately, Suni's excitement was short-lived. Shortly after resuming her training, she fractured her foot, which spurred an ankle injury.

I should just be done, she thought, fighting the urge again to quit the sport.

But Suni was a fighter. She'd rebounded from disappointment in the past, and she would do it again.

After her fracture healed, Suni eased back into training. The recovery process challenged her physically and mentally, but she felt determined to return to her pre-pandemic form.

Suni had missed out on many typical teenage activities due to her training schedule, but she insisted on attending her high school prom. For the memorable occasion, she wore a stunning backless black dress.

Several months later, the eighteen-year-old graduated from South St. Paul High School. Although she enjoyed some classes, like science, juggling school with full-time gymnastics had challenged her. Now, she could focus 100% on gymnastics.

As the Olympic season neared, Suni and her coaches assembled four routines that she would hopefully perform in Tokyo.

Ultimately, Suni helped craft the most difficult uneven bars routine in the world. Seven difficult release moves were packed into the program.

The Winter Cup marked Suni's first competition in over a year. Still recuperating from her ankle injury, the gymnast competed only on uneven bars and the balance beam.

Like most good coaches, Jess sensed that Suni was battling nerves before the competition. So he tried to allay her anxiety by focusing on the big picture.

"Our goal is not to win a meet," Jess reminded her. "Our goal is not to hit a score. Our goal is to get better."

Suni's practices went well. However, she still felt jittery, so she called her father.

"I'm nervous," she confided to him.

John knew how to alleviate his daughter's nerves.

"Have fun," he told her. "Do well for yourself, not for anyone else."

Later that day, Suni unveiled her spectacular uneven bars set. She performed the complex routine with a graceful fluidity.

"So effortless," remarked gymnastics legend Nastia Liukin.

"She is stellar," 1984 Olympic champion Tim Daggett added.

Suni returned home, feeling pleased with her effort. She celebrated by watching her favorite television shows like *The Vampire Diaries* and *Fuller House*.

Suni competes at the Olympic Trials.

At one point, the teenager became hooked on Netflix's reality show, *The Circle*. Part social experiment/part competition, the series featured contestants striving to win a popularity contest with a $100,000 prize.

Suni was disappointed when she finished binging the show. Eager for more episodes, the teenager sampled the Brazilian version of the show.

Suni also enjoyed watching *Lucifer*. She recommended the drama series about the first fallen angel to all her friends.

"It's really good," she told them. "You should watch it."

Suni even starred in her own television show. She was featured in Peacock's original series, *Golden: The Journey of USA's Elite Gymnasts*. The show followed five Olympic team contenders: Suni, Laurie Hernandez, Morgan Hurd, Konnor McClain, and MyKayla Skinner.

Before long, it was time to fly to Fort Worth, Texas, for the 2021 U.S. Championships. A strong showing would enhance Suni's status as a favorite to make the Olympic team.

Suni was thrilled to learn that her father made the trip. It would be his first time watching her compete in person since his accident.

At the conclusion of the U.S. Championships, Suni was the all-around silver medalist for a second straight year. Once again, she finished behind her idol, Simone.

Suni also successfully defended her gold medal on the uneven bars and collected a silver medal on the balance beam.

"This was a really good confidence booster because I wasn't even at my full potential on floor," she remarked. "I'm really proud of myself."

Thanks to her strong finish, Suni qualified for the 2021 Olympic Trials. The hardworking gymnast burst into tears of joy. She was so close to realizing her dream.

U.S. Olympic Team Trials ad featuring Suni Lee

St. Louis, Missouri, played host for the 2021 Olympic Trials. Suni knew a strong showing would land her on the U.S. team.

On the first day of competition, a nervous Suni FaceTimed her parents for another pep talk. Her nerves were bubbling over.

"I'm nervous," Suni confessed. "I'm going to throw up."

John calmed his daughter's anxiety with his elegant, inspiring words. When they said their goodbyes, Suni had recovered her confidence. She felt ready to fight for a spot on the Olympic team.

"I want to do it for my family and coaches obviously, but I also want to do it for myself," she told *People*. "I've just been through so much."

The Olympic Trials took place at The Dome at America's Center. Even in the cavernous arena, Suni could hear Shyenne screaming her support from the stands. She loved to pick out a loved one's voice in a packed audience.

In the end, Suni finished second behind Simone. Interestingly, she had the highest second-day total of any gymnast. She became the first gymnast in eight years to outscore Simone in a one-day all-around score!

At the conclusion of the event, Suni, Simone, Grace McCallum, and Jordan Chiles were named to the four-member Olympic team. Additionally, Jade Carey and MyKayla Skinner won spots as individual competitors.

"I feel really relieved and very emotional," Suni said following the meet. "It's surreal to say I am an Olympian. Hopefully, when I go back to the hotel, I will be able to talk to my family."

Suni couldn't believe it when gymnastics legend Shannon Miller officially announced her as an Olympian in a ceremony after the competition. She scanned the crowd for her family and spotted her parents weeping with joy.

Then, Suni wiped away her own tears.

"To just be an inspiration to other Hmong people means a lot to me too."

Suni's life became a whirlwind of activity after being named to the Olympic team. She appeared with her teammates on NBC's *Today* show, posed for photoshoots, attended team meetings, and participated in several media sessions.

Suni was the first Hmong American Olympian, a distinction that filled her with pride. She hoped to inspire other Hmong people to pursue their dreams.

"Competing for the Hmong community is important for me," she told *TeamUSA.org*. "I think a lot of people in the Hmong community also are afraid to branch out and do sports and continue with it. I want to be someone that inspires them to do it."

Many Hmong women were thrilled to witness Suni flourish in her sport because they'd not pursued their favorite sport when they were younger.

Hmong Gaocher Yang, a former high school athlete became emotional when she watched Suni compete at the Olympic Trials.

"It was emotional because, in my generation, I feel our parents didn't see the value of sports, so to see that after our generation is just amazing," she told *KMSP News*.

In fact, Yang hoped that Suni would inspire other girls to play a sport.

"I think it will be an inspiration," Yang added. "I think it will open their vision, their eyes to [see] that they are able to pursue those types of dreams and that it is possible."

"Suni is this breath of fresh air and hope and light," activist Tou Ger Xiong said. "It's something positive we can celebrate in our Hmong community—not only in Minnesota but across the country."

Sometimes Suni would be grocery shopping with her mom, and a member of the Hmong community would stop her to say they were proud of her.

The teenager felt honored to be admired and supported by her Hmong peers. She took her responsibility as a role model seriously.

"As a proud Hmong-American, I'm trying to spread positivity about Hmong people," she told *The New York Times*.

Suni had become a local celebrity in the Twin Cities! And with the Olympics on the horizon, her star might shine even brighter one day.

St. Paul shows their support for Suni.

"I want to be one of the best in the world, but I also want to succeed for my family."

Following a resurgence of COVID-19 breakouts, the International Olympic Committee and organizers for the Tokyo Games barred fans from attending Olympic events.

Suni was crushed that her family would miss seeing her compete in person in Tokyo. Her parents were equally disappointed, having already purchased their plane tickets months earlier.

Although Suni's parents wouldn't travel to Japan, they showed their support for their daughter in other ways. Her folks hosted a fundraiser to cover her spending needs in Tokyo. They sold over one thousand autographed Team Suni t-shirts to local community members eager to support the gymnast.

"I am proud," Suni's father told *People*. "The family's proud. The community is very proud of her."

Suni, Simone, Grace, and Jordan arrived at the 2021 Olympics as the gold medal favorites for the team event. The American gymnasts stayed in a Tokyo hotel rather than in the Olympic Village, which some athletes found too distracting.

On July 25, Suni and her teammates marched into the Ariake Gymnastics Centre to begin their Olympic competition. For qualifications, the girls wore navy blue leotards with red stars decorating the body and sleeves. The design signified fireworks on the Fourth of July.

To complement her patriotic leotard, Suni donned white acrylic nails bearing the Olympics rings.

With her family and friends watching live at a viewing party in Minnesota, Suni and her teammates sailed through the team competition's qualifying round.

Suni earned spots in three individual event finals: the women's all-around, balance beam, and uneven bars.

On day two of the team competition, the Americans resembled superheroes in their red-sleeved leotards with a white band across the chest and a blue bottom. A whopping 7,600 Swarovski crystals were sprinkled across the leotard's front, back, and sleeves to add sparkle and glam to their look.

The American women began their quest for gold on vault. Suni was not competing on the apparatus, so she cheered her teammates from the sidelines.

Grace and Jordan performed solid vaults, but Simone struggled with her effort. Becoming disoriented during her flip in the air, Simone downgraded a planned 2.5 twists to 1.5 and landed awkwardly.

It was revealed that Simone suffered from the twisties, a terrifying state of disassociation that inhibits athletes from completing a skill. Nearly every elite gymnast has dealt with the condition at some point in their career. Unfortunately for Simone, she got the twisties at the Olympic Games.

Concerned for her safety, Simone left the floor with the team doctor to discuss her options. The gymnastics legend knew she could risk serious injury if she competed. She needed to withdraw from the competition.

When Simone returned to the arena, her teammates were warming up for round two, the uneven bars. The team captain gathered the Americans for a quick meeting and informed them of her decision to withdraw.

Suni and Simone are interviewed by NBC.
(NBC)

"I'm sorry," she told her teammates. "I love you guys, but you're gonna be just fine. You guys have trained your whole entire life for this; it's fine. I've been to an Olympics. I'll be fine. This is your first—you go out there and kick ass, okay?"

Initially, the girls seemed shaken by the news. However, they quickly regrouped and focused on their pursuit of an Olympic medal.

After changing into her warmup suit, Simone became the team's unofficial cheerleader. She even volunteered to be an errand girl if her teammates needed anything.

Despite the distraction of losing their star gymnast, Grace performed a strong uneven bars routine with a stuck landing on her dismount. Jordan, a last-minute substitute for Simone, followed with a clutch performance of her own.

Finally, Suni closed out the uneven bars segment with one of the best routines of her life. She scored a whopping 15.4.

"Going up to perform that bar routine was the most pressure I've ever felt in my life," she admitted later. "I told myself to do what I normally do and just swing. Because if I put all that pressure on myself, I probably would have fallen...I just tried not to think about the fact that Simone wasn't competing or anything else."

Going into the third rotation, the Americans trailed Russia by 2.5 points. They would face the intimidating balance beam next.

When Grace delivered a shaky routine, Suni couldn't afford any errors. Thankfully, she was the picture of composure, earning a 14.133 for her efforts. Jordan finished the rotation with a stellar beam routine of her own.

The American girls had gained ground on the Russians and trailed them by .08 of a point. The gold medal would be decided on the final rotation, floor exercise.

As the first American to compete, Grace's solid tumbling was marred by a step out on her second tumbling pass. Despite the error, she earned a respectable 13.500 from the judges.

Jordan followed with a troubled routine. She sailed out of bounds on a tumbling pass and fell on another. With a score of 11.700, the Americans would not capture gold.

Suni hadn't planned to compete on the floor exercise in the finals. A last-minute substitute for Simone, she hadn't even warmed up any tumbling.

A fierce competitor, Suni pushed all doubts from her mind and concentrated on delivering a solid floor routine. Maybe the Americans wouldn't be draped in gold at the end of the night, but they could still wear silver or bronze.

Suni competes in the Olympic team final.
(Ricardo Bufolin)

Once again, Suni rose to the challenge. Her floor exercise struck the perfect balance of athleticism and artistry. It was more than enough to capture a silver medal for Team USA.

The Russian girls squealed exuberantly when the final standings showed them as the winners. Meanwhile, Great Britain surprised many gymnastics pundits by claiming the bronze medal.

Suni, Simone, Grace, and Jordan were all smiles when they received their silver medals. Although they'd hadn't captured gold, they were still proud of their accomplishment.

Following the event, the press descended on Simone Biles with questions. What had caused the G.O.A.T. to withdraw from the team final? Would she compete in the remaining events?

"I just felt like it would be a little bit better to take a back seat, work on my mindfulness," Simone explained. "I knew that the girls would do an absolutely great job. And I didn't want to risk the team a medal for kind of my screwups because they've worked way too hard for that. So, I just decided that those girls need to go and do the rest of our competition."

Suni's tweet summarized her feelings on the Americans' finish: "Never been prouder to be a part of such an amazing team with an amazing group of girls. We stepped up when we needed to and did this for ourselves. We do not owe anyone a gold medal. We are winners in our hearts."

Suni also posted a photo of the Americans celebrating their silver medals. She captioned the image: The Fighting 4.

Team Final Medal Ceremony
(Ricardo Bufolin)

"When people just think of me as a specialist, it's kind of hard because I train so hard on all the other events."

Following a workout the next morning, Simone discovered she still hadn't recovered from the twisties. Thus, the team captain made the agonizing decision to withdraw from the women's all-around. Jade Carey would join Suni in representing the United States in the event.

With Simone's withdrawal, Suni became a top contender for the all-around title. Rebeca Andrade from Brazil and the Russian Olympic Committee's Angelina Melnikova and Vladislava Urazova were also gold medal candidates.

Now the top American in the all-around competition, Suni received the lion's share of media attention. Television cameras chronicled her every move as she prepared for the biggest meet of her life.

"Just do your thing," Jess told her as she walked to her first event, vault.

Determined as ever, Suni completed a powerful Yurchenko double twist with beautiful air position and only a tiny hop on the landing. It was one of the best vaults she'd ever competed. Her stellar effort earned her a 14.600.

For round two, Suni performed a complex uneven bars routine that was nearly flawless. The judges awarded the program with a 15.300

Midway through the competition, Rebeca Andrade held first place. Suni sat behind her in second, and Angelina Melnikova occupied third place.

Suni faced the balance beam in her third round. She calmed her nerves by giving herself an internal pep talk during her routine. Her breathtaking performance featured just a slight wobble on a triple wolf turn. When 13.833 flashed on the scoreboard, Suni looked pleased with her score.

With one event remaining, Suni had claimed the top position in the standings. To stay in first place, she needed to nail the floor exercise.

Because her left ankle still bothered her, Suni opted not to perform a fourth tumbling pass. Just that morning, Jess had created new choreography for the routine to make up for the exclusion.

Suni handled the last-minute changes like a seasoned veteran. The lyrical gymnast performed the piece as if she'd known it her whole life. She delivered the best floor exercise of her Olympics and earned a score of 13.700.

With her work completed, Suni waited to see what color medal she would earn. She was assured of at least a silver medal.

Rebeca Andrade controlled her fate. If she scored higher than 13.801, she would claim the gold medal. Anything lower, and Suni would win the all-around event.

As it turned out, Rebeca looked shaky throughout her final routine. She committed two significant errors in her floor exercise by stepping out of bounds twice.

When Rebeca's 13.666 score appeared on the scoreboard, Suni shrieked excitedly. She had won the gold medal.

By finishing second, Rebecca became the first gymnast from Brazil to win an Olympic medal. Meanwhile, Russia's Angelina Melnikova took home the bronze.

Suni competes in the Olympic all-around final.
(Ricardo Bufolin)

A jubilant Suni hugged Jess in celebration. She joined an impressive list of Olympic all-around champions, including Larisa Latynina, Nadia Comaneci, Mary Lou Retton, Nastia Liukin, Gabby Douglas, and Simone Biles.

From the stands, Suni's teammates showered her with cheers and a standing ovation. Gymnasts on the floor lined up to offer her congratulatory hugs.

With her victory, Suni became the fifth straight American to take home Olympic all-around gold. She was also the first Asian American to win the title.

"When I saw my score come out on top, it was so emotional," Suni recalled. "It doesn't feel like real life."

Back in Minnesota, Suni's family and friends celebrated her victory. Their support meant the world to the gymnast.

"My community is so amazing," Suni gushed. "They were all watching together and got to see me win a gold medal."

Many people from the Hmong community don't reach their goals," the new Olympic champion added. "I want them to know you can reach your dreams and don't ever give up."

Olympic ad featuring Suni Lee & Katie Ledecky
(NBC)

"I hope I can inspire people."

Thanks to her inspiring gold medal win, Suni became a breakout star of the Tokyo Olympics. Sports fans clamored to learn more about the American gymnast who had dazzled the world. Media outlets lined up to interview gymnastics' newest superstar.

Following her all-around success, Suni was whisked off to do interviews with media from all over the world.

"It doesn't feel like real life," the overwhelmed teenager remarked.

Shortly after her victory, Suni received flattering news from her hometown. St. Paul honored the gymnast with a Sunisa Lee Day.

On August 1st, Suni returned to the Ariake Gymnastics Centre for the uneven bars final. The first competitor on the apparatus, the American lost her focus early in the routine and missed a few connections.

Ultimately, Belgium's Nina Derwael earned the gold medal with a stellar set. Anastasia Iliankova of the Russian Olympic Committee took runner-up honors, and Suni held on for the bronze.

Suni kept trending on social media platforms too. People dissected everything about the gymnast, from her incredible uneven bars set to her acrylic nails.

Dancing With the Stars: Suni Lee
(ABC/Dancing With the Stars)

When she logged on to *Instagram*, Suni was stunned to discover that she had reached a huge milestone. The famous gymnast had accumulated over a million followers!

Then, to satisfy all her new fans, Suni posted a photo of her kissing her gold medal. She captioned it with *OLYMPIC ALL-AROUND CHAMPION. So surreal. I can't thank you all enough for the love and support. Thank you to everyone who has believed in me and never gave up on me. This is a dream come true. WE DID IT.*

Following the Olympics, Suni's life became even busier! She began classes at Auburn University, made personal appearances, and appeared on several talk shows.

Suni was thrilled when the producers of *Dancing With the Stars* asked her to appear on their show. She was paired with Sasha Farber and quickly became one of the viewers' favorite contestants, thanks to her versatility across many musical genres.

Suni Lee was enjoying the perks of her success thanks to many years of dedication and hard work. She'd become a role model to many people who admired her across the globe.

When Suni appeared on NBC's *Today*, she was shown a video of an 8-year-old Hmong gymnast who looked up to her. Ever humble, the Olympic champion was moved to tears by the young girl who admired her.

"For people to say that I'm an inspiration is just incredible," Suni remarked.

Suni Lee would have to get used to being a role model. Her story was sure to inspire children for generations to come!

Suni Lee competes with Sasha Farber.
(ABC/Dancing With the Stars)

2021 Olympic Games
Team: 2, All-Around: 1, Uneven Bars: 3, Balance Beam: 5

2021 Olympic Trials
All-Around: 2, Uneven Bars: 1, Balance Beam: 1, Floor Exercise: 9

2021 U.S. Championships
All-Around: 2, Uneven Bars: 1, Balance Beam: 2, Floor Exercise: 5

2021 U.S. Classic
Uneven Bars: 10, Balance Beam: 8

2021 American Classic
Uneven Bars: 1, Balance Beam: 1, Floor Exercise: 5

2021 Winter Cup
Uneven Bars: 1, Balance Beam: 3

2019 World Championships
Team: 1, All-Around: 8, Uneven Bars: 3, Floor Exercise: 2

2019 Worlds Team Selection Camp
All-Around: 2, Vault: 6, Uneven Bars: 1, Balance Beam: 2, Floor Exercise: 2

2019 U.S. Championships
All-Around: 1, Uneven Bars: 1, Balance Beam: 4, Floor Exercise: 3

2019 U.S. Classic
Uneven Bars: 2, Balance Beam: 8

2019 American Classic
Uneven Bars: 5, Balance Beam: 2

2019 City of Jesolo Trophy
Team: 1, All-Around: 1, Uneven Bars: 1, Balance Beam: 3, Floor Exercise: 1

2018 U.S. Championships (Junior)
All-Around: 3, Vault: 6, Uneven Bars: 1, Balance Beam: 2, Floor Exercise: 5

2018 U.S. Classic (Junior)
All-Around: 5, Vault: 24, Uneven Bars: 3, Balance Beam: 1, Floor Exercise: 25

2018 Pacific Rim Championships (Junior)
Team: 1, Vault: 2, Balance Beam: 2, Floor Exercise: 2

2017 U.S. Championships (Junior)
All-Around: 8, Vault: 17, Uneven Bars: 6, Balance Beam: 11, Floor Exercise: 5

2017 U.S. Classic (Junior)
Balance Beam: 10, Floor Exercise: 4

2017 International Gymnmix (Junior)
Team: 1, Uneven Bars: 2

2016 U.S. Championships (Junior)
All-Around: 10, Vault: 23, Uneven Bars: 10, Balance Beam: 20, Floor Exercise: 5

2016 U.S. Classic (Junior)
All-Around: 16, Vault: 34, Uneven Bars: 22, Balance Beam: 15, Floor Exercise: 6

2015 Hopes Championships (Junior)
All-Around: 1, Vault: 6, Uneven Bars: 2, Balance Beam: 2

Essential Links

Twitter
twitter.com/sunisalee

Instagram
instagram.com/sunisalee

TikTok
tiktok.com/@sunisalee

NBC Olympics Athlete Profile
nbcolympics.com/athletes/sunisa-lee-1651746

Auburn University Gymnastics
auburntigers.com/sports/womens-gymnastics

USA Gymnastics
usagym.org

Midwest Gymnastics
midwestgymnastics.com

Author Page
www.christinedzidrums.com

About the Author

Christine Dzidrums has written biographies on many inspiring personalities: ***Clayton Kershaw, Mike Trout, Yuna Kim, Shawn Johnson, Nastia Liukin, The Fierce Five, Gabby Douglas, Sutton Foster, Kelly Clarkson, Idina Menzel*** and ***Missy Franklin***. Christine's first Young Adult novel, ***Cutters Don't Cry***, won a Moonbeam Children's Book Award. Her follow-up to ***Cutters***, ***Kaylee: The "What If?" Game***, won a gold medal at the Children's Literary Classic Awards. She also wrote the tween book ***Fair Youth*** and the beginning reader books ***Future Presidents Club*** and the ***Princess Dessabelle*** series. Her most recent work is the YA novel, ***But I'm Eponine***. Ms. Dzidrums lives in Southern California with her husband and three children.

www.ChristineDzidrums.com
@ChristineWriter.

Now sports fans can learn about gymnastics' greatest stars! Americans **Shawn Johnson** and **Nastia Liukin** became the darlings of the 2008 Beijing Olympics when the fearless gymnasts collected 9 medals between them. Four years later at the 2012 London Olympics, America's **Fab Five** claimed gold in the team competition. A few days later, **Gabby Douglas** added another gold medal to her collection when she became the fourth American woman in history to win the Olympic all-around title. The *GymnStars* series reveals these gymnasts' long, arduous path to Olympic glory. *Gabby Douglas: Golden Smile, Golden Triumph* received a **2012 Moonbeam Children's Book Award**.

Theater fans first fell for **Sutton Foster** in her triumphant turn as *Thoroughly Modern Millie*. Since then the triple threat has charmed Broadway audiences by playing a writer, a princess, a movie star, a nightclub singer, and a Transylvania farm girl. Now the two-time Tony winner is conquering television in the acclaimed series *Bunheads*. A children's biography, ***Sutton Foster: Broadway Sweetheart, TV Bunhead*** details the role model's rise from a tiny ballerina to the toast of Broadway and Hollywood.

Idina Menzel's career has been "Defying Gravity" for years! With starring roles in *Wicked* and *Rent*, the Tony-winner is one of theater's most beloved performers. The powerful vocalist has also branched out in other mediums. She has filmed a recurring role on television's smash hit *Glee* and lent her talents to the Disney films, *Enchanted* and *Frozen*. A children's biography, ***Idina Menzel: Broadway Superstar*** narrates the actress' rise to fame from a Long Island wedding singer to overnight success!

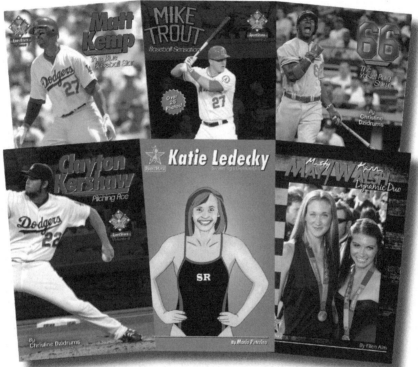

SportStars focuses on the world's most successful and influential athletes. ***Matt Kemp: True Blue Baseball Star*** tells the story of one of the Dodgers most successful players in history. ***Mike Trout: Baseball Sensation*** chronicles the New Jersey native's rise from a toddler running the base paths to winning the 2012 American League Rookie of the Year Award. A children's biography, ***66: The Yasiel Puig Story*** will help young readers learn about the man behind the baseball legend. ***Clayton Kershaw: Pitching Ace*** is the latest title in the ***SportsStars Series***!

Fair Youth
Emylee of Forest Springs

Twelve-year-old Emylee Markette has felt invisible her entire life. Then one fateful afternoon, three beautiful sisters arrive in her sleepy New England town and instantly become the most popular girls at Forest Springs Middle School. To everyone's surprise, the Fay sisters befriend Emylee and welcome her into their close-knit circle. Before long, the shy loner finds herself running with the cool crowd, joining the track team and even becoming friends with her lifelong crush.

Through it all, though, Emylee's weighed down by nagging suspicions. Why were the Fay sisters so anxious to befriend her? How do they know some of her inner thoughts? What do they truly want from her?

When Emylee eventually discovers that her new friends are secretly fairies, she finds her life turned upside down yet again and must make some life-changing decisions.

Fair Youth: Emylee of Forest Springs marks the first volume in an exciting new book series.

Lyric Teague thinks she's the perfect girl to play
the doomed Eponine in her high school production of ***Les
Misérables***. After all, for the past three years, she has survived
the agony of loss and the pain of unrequited love. But the teenager quickly learns that her drama teacher and the other kids see
her in an entirely different way. As opening night approaches,
Lyric must determine for herself whether she's a tragic victim or
a beautiful heroine who inspires a rebellion.

The SoCal Series

Cutters Don't Cry
2010 Moonbeam Children's Book Award Winner!
In a series of raw journal entries written to her absentee father, a teenager chronicles her penchant for self-harm, a serious struggle with depression and an inability to vocally express her feelings.

Kaylee: The 'What If?' Game
"I play the 'What If?'" game all the time. It's a cruel, wicked game."When free spirit Kaylee suffers a devastating loss, her personality turns dark as she struggles with depression and unresolved anger. Can Kaylee repair her broken spirit, or will she remain a changed person?

Made in the USA
Columbia, SC
09 January 2022